CATITUDES & PLATITUDES

Select Titles also by Susan Wingate

CATITUDES & PLATITUDES

SUSAN WINGATE

Roberts Press

Seattle

2016

Roberts Press
An imprint of False Bay Books
www.robertspress.com
Seattle, Washington 98126

USA

First published by Roberts Press, 2016

The poem, The Dance of Wind in Trees, was previously published in the Virginia Quarterly Online.

Wingate, Susan.
[Poems, Selections]
Catitudes & Platitudes : poems / Susan Wingate
pages   cm
ISBN 978-0-9898078-5-2 (paperback)
1. Title

Printed in the United States of America

Designed by Awesome Book Designs

For Bob

Contents

catitudes & platitudes

BURIED TREASURE

And the loamy ground gave up easily against
the tip of my shovel.
My foot barely needing weight.
And the treasure lay waiting to be returned to
its place
(so close to the spot where I'd found my
treasure)
Among the roots and rocks below the surface of
the ground.
The treasure I'd held for eighteen years needed
returning.
And I dived in with the treasure after laying it
down inside the hole I dug.
The hole under the sprawling alder that leans
out into the yard—arms reaching for my
treasure.
As a gift. As a gift.
The earth felt cool and gritty against my cheek.
The grass flecking my skin with bits of green
and yellow.
And face-to-face with my treasure
Water gushed into the hole.
Water springing from the soul, from a single
cloud so full—a water balloon
dropped from a high window,
Exploding and breaking on the ground.

SPRING

At the back end
Of a drawn out
Solstice twilight
Months long and lasting
A blue iris sky blinks
The sleep from her eyes
And kisses
the earth's baby mouth

THE HOUSE WHERE CATS GO

I visited, last night, the house where cats go.
Its walls are smooth stucco and white and it sits
on a hill with a chain-link fence that guards it.
The chain-link fence cuts off entrance from
people who want to go inside.
And a flat black road climbs the hill and trims
the row of houses and a set of concrete steps
trims the road.
Cats there play together in this house.
They get in and out by way of a sprawling oak
tree that sits, mashed, in front of the chain-link
fence.
And when the cats are outside of the fence, they
lead you to other houses with other cats and
yards of grass.
Those houses have a few dogs too.
And the house on the hill has cats of all ages
and sizes.
The fat black one, as black as Midnight, bumps
her butt down the steps that trim the road.
The calico who was chunky but is now smooth
and creamy sits high above on the top of the
stairs.
Another one with fur dark like Razberry Jam in
a jar.
And there are kittens all around, playing, who I
didn't recognize.
Not at first.

Then, remembered from long ago how they'd gotten into poison that Carl had put in the shed even before I lived there.
How they convulsed until they died.
How I didn't know what to do.
But there they were! Well and happy and still kittens. Playing.
None of the cats said a word but they knew me. I knew them. I know how to talk to my cats.
And I hope I get to come back to the house where cats go and to talk with them again. To sit in front of the chain-link fence.
To tell them how much I miss them. How much I remember them.
And to watch them live there in the house where they've gone.

THE DANCE OF WIND IN TREES

cha-cha pines dance the can-can
lifting their skirts into the wind

a deer, protected by the loden umbrella, winces,
chews her cud,
twists her head embarrassed for the pines

one tree drops a cone--scudding over brown
leaves and needles,
near the deer,
stirring her and
making her gawk at the vulgar swerve-y
branches
swaying seductively above her,
demanding notice.

ON A MOURNING SUCH AS THIS

Through a misty mourning such as this,
crisp as vellum,
our sun beheads the horizon,
guillotines the crystal mantle.
A shard of bloody iodine
(against a blue vein of beckoning hope)
mushrooms, contracts
—splits the seconds
—fractures fractals.
Blinded.
Her hands held out in awe,
fingers shuttering the phantasm unfurling.
Rallying,
digging for a glimmer,
of understanding and understanding nothing
before light breaks the dawn
she rubs an opal from each lash
gathering them into her palm.

FAMILY TIES

For what? She asks the sky.
You mustn't fret.
The wind knows the answer.
(the sky married the wind).
The rain sibling meets up now and again
Reminding of familial traits,
Of heritage,
Of differences.
Old snow shows her gray face with wisdom
Each wrinkle holds ancient gen,
History harkens to her youth
Who snub her—
Fiery.
Absolute.
This is my time, she bays.
As snow retreats, hurt.
Embarrassed.
Only to return
with her offerings of
unwelcome advice.

ONE SLEEPY WOMAN...

...has questions about the coming of day
and its falling away... they go:

Were dusk and dawn created for morning's
first open eye,
For her, the drowsy one leaning on the counter?
coming up slow and in a season will go.
A sinful ebb,
An atoning flow?

Forget the crappy rhyming and listen: her
questions continue...

Will no other creature traversing this land
Give a hoot about such a fading in or out?
Or will they care if a light brushes the
morning?
–Charred, grayed, grayer, ashen blue—
Cheeky moves toward some goal line,
warping into a golden hue
Splashing onward in iodine drifts
—modern art on a Neapolitan canvas.

And what about those tree skeletons in the
horizon?
Will they rise again from winter's grave?
As they chill under tatty sweaters
Dropping their towels – sluts for warmer days

Stripping naked for the hotty, for summer's
gaze—

Summer, ah, summer!
Some have seen,
toe-to-toe with dusk and dawn
So intimate, so scandalous
—a salute and a bump of the hip, a wink for one
final fling.

And who will care but Ms. sleepy-eyes—she,
witness to such adulteries?
Will they, flora or mountain?
Will they, building or car?

Might the sleeper,
With saggy wet eyes watching the trysts—
nearing and parting,
Sloping out of sun
slipping into moon
One sexy Hello
One haggard goodbye
Promiscuity at its best, fickle at worst—
In her tie-dye way, who gabbles, "for now."
Thanking Jesus she's not sinful, day and night,
night and day.
Till sleeping eyes—bowls of pudding...

Blink.

THE UNSPOKEN CHILD

When the unspoken child takes her leave
A robin's life ends against a crystal pane
When a voice quivers out one final goodbye,
Mud pools in concentric meaningless time.

When the old man comforts his own child
Tears brim his white eyes, urns pouring from
his marble hands
When his stone fingers can't feel her
Chalk etched in wet sand.

When unfair miles separate them
A black X on the datebook
When life un-clings its fragile fingers
We cry for an unspoken child.

THE BEGINNING OF EVERYDAY

Again, this morning (makes 5 days in a row
now), four baby rats trapped inside the oat bin,
hopping, screeching, "Lady! Lady! Help us!"

I tip the bin forward letting the babies scamper
around dodging my feet, complaining of
hardships and scary dark quarters. Worrying
about Bootsie, the grey & black tabby with
socks rolled up to her elbows meant for the hard
work of chasing rats. The babies drill down into
a fresh mound of earth seeking shelter. Still. I
watch. Amused.

A deer stomps with impatient cloven hooves,
hungry for the oats I'm holding in a big silver
bowl, where the rats got caught, in sweet meal,
in green mineral pellets supplied for winter's
puny array of shrubby food.

My mornings start out this way. A humor of
creatures--of three hungry raccoon, a curled cat
asleep on the back porch chair (the one with a
fake wool heating pad). A white dog smiles—
bubble gum gums—aching to get past my legs,
through the door where he might give hunt—
there's that raccoon, you see.
That one. Sitting on the barn-wood fence.

A GOOSY LESSON ON EGG BEAKS

My backyard is black and white under a fatter
moon

The moon paints images
Effects in vivid, or sepia and tonight we're all
about stark

A phosphorous goose careens over in a shimmer
of pewter sky and honks: audio files from an
old fashioned car cartoon and Mr. Magoo with
bottle-bottom glasses driving aimless routes—
He knows not what he does, just plows on, "oh
my, oh my," through the night

Like this goose, she scatters between the greater
swarm of geese — waxy white against satin
flowing like a prom queen's skirt — and that
moon winking at her and wishing the birds
souther, more souther where warm weather
lives

I wonder why the goose doesn't simply fly
away? Away, away, led away by the chiffon
moon? But I take a gander. Her mate, a fat blue
boy in a top hat waiting on a pond with eggs in
the shallows. He honks their affair settling
there, there in the shallows before winter sets
and pickles their wanting of more.

More what? More good weather? More bad?
More hatchlings? Food?

And me, worrying on the goose chicks, with
those egg beaks hooked in, breaking their shells,
breaking out of their calcium jails—from
suffocating if they don't

Then, grown and gone before I know. Are any
left on the nest?

And the nested left lay dead.
Born with no egg beak.
Banging it out and getting nowhere, feeling the
outer shell but caught inside,
They cannot break out.

LOVER MOON

A slingshot moon,
We'll call him Lover Moon,
Aiming for his luv-a, he calls her,
Gropes for an ashen sky
Stilling his hand
Ice on his wrist
Chilling Mr. Cosmos
His ethos chilled along.
On a rock propelled toward
The lover, a star of the night shows,
Remains at arm's length
Distant as any planet from any other planet
Flashes her bright smile
And glides ahead of him,
Her flashy skirt billowing,
Knowing her Lover Moon will follow.

BEAR DREAMING

We warmed each other.
Me and three bears.
All white.
Momma bear and two of her babies.
Tucked. In the thick of my fur-pillows.
Billowing under head. Lifting and lowering at
each breath.
Sleeping on the road in town.
Movie-goers ignored as they funneled into
theatre.
No one bothered us. They walked around.
People pretended not to notice us lying there on
the ground.
One shady character glanced.
We didn't care.
In our heap of warmth.
Our heap of comfort.
In protection.
We didn't bother with anybody. Nobody.
Lolling there on a sidewalk. In town.
People walking by. On the other side of the
road.
Just we bears. Some 2,000 pounds.
Piled one on top the other.

FOGGY GROGGY MUSIC

There's music in the fog
A nanosecond syncopate
One million drumbeats
Rice Crispy crackling popping

There's music in the fog
delicate misty voices
With fingers touching skin
tapping out a love song of memories unfolding

There's an echo in the fog
A cottony-thick aura
With laundered bed sheets sopping
Dripping ghosties rock n' roll
in rock n' roll bands, with rock n' roll
sunglasses and cigarettes
Balancing a bass
snapping fingertips
Through a fall of ocean spray.

And the music yet to play
Down the road through the valley
Players tapping sultry music, listen to
A Gauzy fog burn away.

CROW WINGS

A wind
whispered over
crows wings
striking black marks
in the summer sky
warning
of early fall
and death
to the high sun.

THE INFALLIBILITY OF FROST ON ROSE PETALS

the infallibility of frost on rose petals
frames the eye's senses
leaves breathless does wanting
soothes harsh magenta
kills a leaf,
strips an armor from a warrior who
kneels before the majesty—one simply
knows as weather whether one
cares of the dimming sky, weather
wins against the rose petal

ODE TO THE DEAD: For T

Let the phone keep ringin'
Let bodies lie
No need for speakin'
It's a time to cry

Let the mail come in
Let it pile up high
Your time was come
I need to say good-bye

Let the cows sway laden
In milk-drenched teat
I'll mourn my loss
My chest I'll beat

Let no one visit
Let no one in
Let no one touch me
Let no one grin

THE FAT CAT

Her arm across her arm
Her purr,
a rhythm gleeful thick sputtering like an
untimed automobile motor,
She moves not ever with suddenness
Or without well-thought intent
Laps and loads of skin
Under layers and lined fur, resembling
somewhere beneath, a tiger, once, maybe,
many years before she became the domestic
queen she is today...
She refuses impetuous acts, they trouble and
bewilder her you can see when her eyes squint
But then a longing fills her and a bobble of
drool lusting for my finger, my hand, my nudge
The cat, the queen, the extremely rotund and
effusively-skinned *Felinus Roundus Maximus*
Watches a fast junco under glass but, when she
checks her sagging pockets,
Finds it impossible to pay for the meal.

ON THE 506 TO PORTLAND

In a cattle car
riding alone,
Sitting alone in a wintry booth

Bent over
Spooning hot brew,
Ghost steam stings her snout.
Gazing at clicking ocean scenes
Through a porthole,
A film gone haywire...

Sees a fisherman up to his chest in waders and
waters,
A woman waving
the queen mother
Waving, frozen to the beach, blindly at
passengers inside the passing train.
A-Chug-chugging, drones, repeats under a
linked caravan, a dialogue –
An old dike's knee replacement and new-found
career in gourd painting, her life on an island,
and tiring trips to and from home there
– tom-tom in a-rhythm.

A tiny boy wearing coveralls covers his ears as
the train's whistle shrieks by.
"BITCH" scrawled red on a wall,
Kitchen-bags piled on back porches in a line of
tattered houses,

A trench coat muzzled old man cupping and
protecting a stubby cigar –
Scattered ashes skirt the rail across the cement
as the train slows for its next stop.

Unmoving, bridled, lost some thirty years back
–
Her best friend Dolly running away before
sunrise,
Leaving a suicide note on a doorstep,
Gone. To Sarasota – to clown school – fleeing
Freeing herself from treacheries unspoken,
of her friend's junkyard existence.

And, how many more hours?
And, how many more miles?
And, why the train? Why the train?

While the train,
the 506,
Beats a drum
down a track
closing in on Portland.

LOVINGAME

Tallow 'n talc streak her nose.
'nother fight—
play piggy on her toes.
His ears done left.
His mouth be gone.
No where they sing no lovin' song.
A game of cribbage
fill up some void.
They scratch the surface,
an itchy 'rhoid.
It grows and seeps and bleeds and pains.
D' lovingame done lost its gain.

SHEEP BY NUMBERS

The final pillow-y sheep
Leapt, arcing over
the meandering Scotty split-rail fence
stopped mid-air

caught in a blinder of my eyes
falling to sleep
density reversed its bend and that sheep
walked up and bleated
"Y'know, I'm not just a number! I have a
name."

And startled my slumber
Rolling me back to one flannel beginning
...1sheep, 2sheep, 3sheep, 4...

How his number escaped me
I do not know...
While I rub a fist into my socket.
the harbingers of woolly sleep
I, with great effort, repeat
Their bounding and bouncing and, yes, their
Prancing
as I worry—the one with a name.

THE ODD THOUGHT

Spank me, she said,
'Cuz my troubled soul needs a good whippin'

While he considered immortality as a cat.

THE ACT OF BALANCE

Peel the mask off my old face
find crazy youth beneath
Beauty - a trick, I know
meant to alarm and disarm
Mirror, mirror when you crack
I let you fall
and spin, spin, spin en pointe
over a broken dance hall floor
and hang on for dear life.

A CHANGE IN SEASONS

falling...
gusts swirl a sky into cotton candy rainbows
stuffy pumpkins
smiling bananas color heart-shaped leaves
falling from skinny arms, once fat with spring
and summer,
drop in a ticker tape parade
The headlines read
"Autumn Returns!"

PRACTICING

Practice sessions happen at times like this,
before appearances
smiling into a reflection
thinking of future conversations
with someone who could become fiction
at any moment
if plans change or cancel

Practicing happy comes after years of rehearsal
during strained relations
smiling at a person who no longer reflects a
love that used to be
thinking of how today might be different
with that someone new, an essay of hope with
her
lying languid among a toss of gentler arms and
legs
if only plans would change or cancel

Practice sessions occur out of nowhere
after the argument
smiling at nothing anymore
thinking of all the fights before
with you, very real and cruel
changing your fury into I'm Sorry
wishing you could vaporize, change that last
barb cancelling it once and for all.

BATTLING NATURE

locking horns
Bucks slam heads vying with nature
huff out warnings and fret
puff out hot steam
and a Junko trills out a frosty call watching
as the musky scent of rutting season closes in
scrambling away one panicked and crippled
Doe
the winner points his thumping groin toward
her
giving chase
Limping scrawny plate-eyed
carrying a foal to term
the thought shrivels up
in her womb
she lumbers off, on three legs
sheltered only by a waning
bank of leggy thistle
away from
his approach.

LOOKING DOWN

She once had hope.
He expected forgiveness
She looks down, won't look into his eyes
because of the embarrassment drilling out from
his gaze,
She's not cracked up... you know the phrase, to
be
Or to meet his expectations.
He doesn't believe in her
His face reflects resentment of eight long years,
he wanted more but she given her max,
he finds fault in her truth, won't believe the
facts.
Forcing the issue he begs her to speak,
But will we ever talk again?
We just did, when we said hello
Will we ever talk more?
I don't know.
And she lets him walk out.
Where he can take his hopes right along with
him, out that door.

ON WRITING

I write with a calico cattail slung across my
keyboard and
Motor-boat purrs stirring morning's breezy
silence
Creamy like honey
in chamomile tea

I write when you sleep and I can't
With visions of ballerinas and horses dancing
across the backstage of my eyes
Not words yet
only images

And I write with nubby fingers and cracked
nails
Tools of expression
Needing no polish needing no buff
raw and tender, sore—unedited.

I write and the world falls away
Cascading into a cataract of droplets
Blinking by, I don't want to miss their
meaning, their point.
Their entirety.

INDIGESTION CAFÉ

coffee foam trimming the rim of my mug
a waft of the almond shard on the table
beckons my snotty nose
almond bits on the keyboard
from pawing at an oily croissant

a full bladder urges me to the ladies room
my stomach bubbling from dinner last night,
a bean burrito enchilada-style, please
and the breve this morning
and nerves,
sure – from my nerves
but also from snarky publishers,
edgy interviewers, a long rainy drive home,
and shoe soggy on the sidewalk dragging a
surrender flag of toilet paper.

IN STILLNESS

The birds have all gone quiet
There's an eagle in a tree
A freezing breath palls the air
A Cybele perched on her willow chair
– a rocking mocking willow chair
Without a care!
Without a care!

And stares past a silver nickel,
At the fare around her seat
Phrygia tithing gifts of food
Abundant at her feet
The plate, her choice of picking,
Somewhere a clock is ticking,
Talking about tick-tock-ticking

One sap snakes slither round the bottom of her
chair,
Her rocking, mocking rocking chair
they bleat a lonesome mewling
to escape her willow lair.

ODE TO A SHORT-TAILED CAT

In a Twinkle...
As you lie there
I am helpless
In words thoughts and action

As you lie there
Like you had so many times before
Content and watching me while I work

As I watch you lie there
My shrinking violet
Disappearing from my sight

A crushing blow
Spears my chest
Showering pain through each limb
Flowing back from my arms
Settling in my heart

Did God not hear when I begged him to give
me your pain?
Did he ignore my trembled call?
All this senseless cruelty
While you lie there dying
My hand on your side.

MOTHER EARTH

sinking deeper in the ground
proven by years—the heat, the cold, the rain or
shine
those apathetic clouds above
hover on a slow conveyor belt,
to one more rendezvous
across the way,
"Down the road a-piece!"

the blue banner
presses me down in the earth
anchoring me
to a thick grass bed
swaddled in
a sodden blanket on
this spinning ball
with blade fingernails raking
my arms, my legs
words bleed out,
"In this spot, please, let me die."

A SUNRISE

blue grey clouds
holding hands in a chain
block the sun
but find
superhuman power
insurmountable
breaking through

a hummingbird rests at hung jars of
sugar water, its threadlike toes so thin I wonder
how they support her when she spits
...away!

amber hues brighten my paper
casting shadows off my hand
while the floor creaks above my head
under the weight of his feet
he's awake making his way
from room to room

and the dog buckles and pukes
I wonder why
he's had nothing to eat
since yesterday afternoon
save that stolen blade of grass

the thrum of a cat purring
eases me as cooing doves sing background first
string and

warm me to the day
and that sun there
hitting my cheek
with fire from the stove
melts away all of my worries.

APPLE TREES & BOMBS

Depth-charge saucers
Aliens and courtesans
Wanting more
Watch and analyze
suspecting
Differences in me,
Differences in you
Why do you think me
Stranger than the beggar
On the corner
Who smokes
Marlboro filters
Singing olden songs
Of wars and the apple trees
Where we sat
With nobody else
In sight
But you
But me
And that war
With its mortar
Breaking walls
Building walls
And today
With our borders
Clanking shut.

I, CHAMELEON

Patchwork chameleon
Lizard shapeshifter
High school days and ways
Slinking between
The crips the dudes the loadies and
The ever-popular student *gov.*

I, the Chameleon,
Shifty, sly
Quick to wit and to flit away
from a maelstrom
Of judging eyes
Surviving
A log-roller
Out of balance, spinning logs with my toes
On brackish water

My shape-shifting pelt lay on the ground
Flimsy, weak after molting
A locust skin clinging to a tree trunk
Like an afterthought, a reminder
Of what used to be, what used to be me
My lizard ways, extinguished left lazy and dry
Baking in the sun
On a hot rock
Fossilized over eons
To be studied later.

FAITHFUL

How faithful,
I was thinking,
Were the geese
Who blocked the road
On the street
Near our house
Coming home

How faithful
Was the gander
Near his mate
On her nest
On a shallow
Grassy mound
Of the roadside

How true
To her heart
As he stood
In the middle
Of that road
As the night
Fell around her

But he stayed
Threat'ning cars
As they honked
Passing near
And the goose

Hissing back in rejoinder

Someone warned
Of a fox
Or a drunk
Racing by
But the warning
Simply slid
Off his feathers

I am told
They are there
Every morning
Every evening
It's their home
There together
Faithfully.

JAPANESE FLOATS (in Haiku)

far below
a glass
blue whale sighs
and bubbles float
up free through the sea

MEASURING UP GOD

Tell me again, when you think God died?
In war? In peace?

Tell me again, when once we thought it okay to
rebuke Him because things were good?

In trouble man cries out
God save me!
God help me!
Making promises unmade while smooth sailing

See, under a blind troubled water lies a crab
devoured by a squid, a starfish extinguished by
the octopus, savages ravaging.
On still water boats float in their ignorant calm
And below havoc wreaks

Tell me again, when we are Godly?
Tell me what you think you know?

How will we measure God?
How will He measure us?
Tell me.
Will we measure through our wars or from our
peace?
Tell me.
Or, will we measure from both?

CRUSADING FOR THE WORD

Headlong down a silo
The reckless, feckless butterfly

Dragged toward a dewdrop
A charm on a splinter of grass

Cartwheeling tumbling a dune
Boozy at the bottom
Onto a swale from
Birth to discovery

Unfurling a thousand-year dream
Tenders bruised and soulful
Unused, idling in neutral
Where nothing happens

SPRING

At the back end
Of a drawn out
Solstice twilight
Months long and lasting
A blue iris sky blinks
The sleep from her eyes
And kisses
the earth baby's mouth

YOUR INTERCONNECTIVITY

Your interconnectivity
Loses something
While you sit alone
Waiting wailing waste-high
In waste
Talking 'bout, "pain, baby!"
Your plenty is empty
You find your dreams
Trampled
Without matter
Substance
Merit
By your own doing,
Baby!
Critical and angry
Your spit drips with spite
Giraffe spinach tobacco
Spewn at your onlooker

ALABASTER – Numero Dos

alabaster,
a trampolining moon
a black setting in ebony,
its stage
throw off mica dreams
and coral eyes flirt
with magnum force
and brawny lies
roll river rocks of ages
across a Sirius countenance
scorned scorched shredded
bolting heaving
garnet
under a Tibetan encampment
held to the sky
plucked off the palm
a Persian promise
on her snakehead shoulder
her hands held high framing
her rock gift
of earth, mica, and gold.

ALABASTER – Numero Uno

an alabaster moon
an iris overexposed
hurtling through
an agate song
a Mitch Miller baton
invisible bouncing
over starry lyric syllables
scrambled in a yolk
of clouds woven
between Mizar and Alioth
between a pepper hot
samba tune
a night in June
an orchestral welkin jig

NEXT TIME

Next thing I do
After I'm done with what I'm doing now
Is relax—put my feet up and watch the sky
circle above in the opposite direction.
The next person I meet
Won't ask me why or when
They'll know from my face
My reasons are pure.
And I am sure the next time I die
My hands will look like cown hands
Pudgy and white but calloused
From working the soil.
From being helpful.
But next time will be the best time.
Proving me the best of me,
A new time when I will
Try my soul on for size...
Next time.

MOVIELAND

my swath of land, 300 feet long, spills into black
green water of the pond.
the scene from my window, a movie scene,
with ducks waggling up for grubs, for tender
roots, paddling, skillful Platypus bills digging
the earth while they play their part.
a villain fox, thrown in, cast for conflict,
approaches slyly, as they do, slyly watching,
wait-fully under a bramble of catch-thorn and
wild rose,
and the fox pounces, in a start, her blocking laid
out by the director, in a splash, a flutter of
feathers.
and one—only one—with its neck turned late
floats in a pond of reed, of rose petals, of blood,
in this action film, rated V for violence,
one I watch with my fingers to my lips.
until the reel ends and the tape flips out of
control.

NOTHING LEFT

I have nothing to offer you and your blind eyes.
Your inert mind shakes my rage.
Your bitter tongue cut a Z on my breast.

I have nothing more for you when your door
closes in my face and I'm left on the step
wondering what pain you feel when you feel
me.

A lazy word dropping off your lip—a missed
string of spit from your spite.
You missed it with your kerchief, the one you
leave me to catch on my finger
like snot dangling from my fingertip.

And your reversal, so contrived, freezes my
heart when you turn to others who don't know
me like I know me
And your cleaver splits me while it remains
lodged in my breastbone.

PEPPER IN MY COFFEE

I put pepper in my coffee
Because it brings more
Spice into my life

I put chestnuts on my beret
And wander outdoors
Attracting squirrels
And birds to eat and sit
My head announcing
My fame and glory
To the kingdom
Of animals

Sometimes I mix things up
And put pepper on my beret
And chestnuts in my coffee
adding spice to birds' and the squirrels' lives
Adding a nutty flavor to my morning brew

Now, look! There's a fish playing between the
nuts
It bobs around inside my cup

And crazier still
I'll put chestnuts on my pepper
And my mug
Balanced on my hat
Atop the chestnuts, atop the spice
And walk like a super model

Through the woods
And read a tree, telling it stories
Acting like a fox, a vixen
Poised and sly

The squirrels and birds
Will try to avoid, will skirt
But will gather anyway to watch
Me flirt
Playing on their stage.

CAT MOON (Could be Alabaster – Numero Tres)

the moon,
a lazy yellow cat eye,
winks in the night
nodding off
swatting
the world
as it swings
moonbeam to moonbeam –
flirting his heavy brow
licking his chops and
sinking into a dusky-sky sleep.

WHEN I AM 88

When I am 88
Just before I die
Before magnets shift
Before poles realign
Will I find my Papeete?
My Garden of Eden
My peace
The place I'll prove
To search my whole life
The whole of my long days.

When I am 88
Before my eyes cloud over
Before my last long sleep
May a heel of bread
Render my tongue of
Persimmon & honey?
May I not want for more
May water
Nourish my soul like amrita
And quench my parched mind
filling me so I'll
Ask for nothing more.

EXISTING

I can only breathe
In saturation
Of soul, spirit, mind & body
If a canvas
I'd be thick with oil
If a hospital
sick with the quick and dying

I can live only
Under a mantle of thick earth
That fills my lungs
As water fills fish gills
As air fills pockets of robin bones
As rocks in quarries and
Pocks in epidemic proportions

I can only think
When silence has engulfed me
When chatter takes its leave
And atoms scatter
Leaving me gladder
Exponentially...
Forever...
Alone...
Without remorse or excuse.

ABOUT THE AUTHOR

Susan Wingate is a novelist, a poet and a playwright. She lives on an island in the State of Washington where she writes full-time.

You can find all of Susan Wingate's work at her website, www.susanwingate.com.

You can follow Susan on Facebook and Twitter,

www.facebook.com/authorsusanwingate

www.twitter.com/susanwingate

GIVING THANKS

Susan Wingate would like to thank Terry Persun who encouraged her to write this small sampling of her poetry. But, mostly, she wants to thank her husband who tirelessly supports her.